Our

Magical Trip

Planner

Vacation Planner Paris Parks Edition

First Edition May 2020

Paris Parks Edition

© 2019 Our Magical Trip Planner

Our Disneyland Paris Trip

Trip Date:

Duration of Nights:

Special Occasions:

Guest Travelling:

Why we are taking this magical trip:

_____

_____

_____

_____

_____

_____

_____

_____

Travel Details

Flight Details – Date:

Flight Departure Airport:

Flight Time and Flight No.:

Via Stopover Airport:

Layover Time:

Arrival Time Local:

Eurostar Details – Date:

Train Departure Station:

Train Time and Booking No.:

Arrival Time Local:

Euro Tunnel Details - Date:

Booking time and No.:

From Location:

Arrival Time Local:

Travel Details

Flight Details – Date:

Flight Departure Airport:

Flight Time and Flight No.:

Via Stopover Airport:

Layover Time:

Arrival Time Local:

Eurostar Details – Date:

Train Departure Station:

Train Time and Booking No.:

Arrival Time Local:

Euro Tunnel Details - Date:

Booking time and No.:

From Location:

Arrival Time Local:

Driving Details

Route Plans: Date:

Starting Location and Time:

Starting Time:

Stops:

Arrival Location and Time:

Route Specifics (Petrol, Tolls)

_____

_____

_____

Route Plans: Date:

Starting Location and Time:

Starting Time:

Stops:

Arrival Location and Time:

Route Specifics (Petrol, Tolls)

_____

_____

_____

Driving Details

Route Plans: Date:

Starting Location and Time:

Starting Time:

Stops:

Arrival Location and Time:

Route Specifics (Petrol, Tolls)

_____

_____

_____

Route Plans: Date:

Starting Location and Time:

Starting Time:

Stops:

Arrival Location and Time:

Route Specifics (Petrol, Tolls)

_____

_____

_____

Accommodation Details

Accommodation Name:

Check in Date and Time:

Address:_____

_____

Check Out Time:

Hotel Amenities:

Notes:

Accommodation Name:

Check in Date and Time:

Address:_____

_____

Check Out Time:

Hotel Amenities:

Notes:

Accommodation Details

Accommodation Name:

Check in Date and Time:

Address:_____

_____

Check Out Time:

Hotel Amenities:

Notes:

Accommodation Name:

Check in Date and Time:

Address:_____

_____

Check Out Time:

Hotel Amenities:

Notes:

Notes

_____
_____
_____
_____
_____
_____
_____
_____
_____
_____
_____
_____
_____
_____
_____
_____
_____
_____
_____
_____

Notes

_____
_____
_____
_____
_____
_____
_____
_____
_____
_____
_____
_____
_____
_____
_____
_____
_____
_____
_____

Vacation Costings

Holiday Budget £$€

Cost Breakdown

Travel Costs:

Flight Cost Total: £$€

Eurostar / Tunnel: £$€

Train Costs: £$€

Transfer Cost: £$€

Car Hire Cost: £$€

Petrol / Tolls Costs: £$€

Accommodation Costs:

Accommodation 1: £$€

Accommodation 2: £$€

Accommodation 3: £$€

Accommodation 4: £$€

Accommodation Parking Total: £$€

Park Ticket Costs:

- Disney Tickets   £$€

- Other Tickets   £$€

- Theme Park Car Park Costs: £$€

Dining Costs (Off Site):

- Food Money Per Day: £$€

- Snack Money Per Day: £$€

- Supermarket Shops: £$€

Other Spending:

- Souvenirs: £$€

- Retail Shopping: £$€

Saving Initiatives

Money to save per month:

Cost Cutting Initiatives:

(Examples: Ditch the Starbucks Coffees, make lunch pack ups, cut back on eating out, switch to supermarket brands)

_____
_____
_____
_____

_____
_____
_____
_____

_____
_____
_____
_____

Set your budget and divide by the number of weeks you will save over, colour a mouse in each time you have deposited that weekly amount.

Mouse Savings

Total Savings Goal: _____   ⬤ = _____

Notes

_____
_____
_____
_____
_____
_____
_____
_____
_____
_____
_____
_____
_____
_____
_____
_____
_____
_____
_____
_____

Disneyland Paris App

Visit
https://www.disneylandparis.com/
for information for before you arrive
at the park, park maps and more
information on the new Fastpass
systems that Paris has in place.

Download the Disneyland Paris App. This will be
your tool for booking Fastpasses, checking wait
times, view where you are on the map, and even
buy your tickets just ahead of your visit and
scan your phone for entrance at the gate.

Disney Meal Plans

For Disney on-site guest you can purchase, or book offers that come with a Disney Meal Plan.

The benefits of a Disney Meal Plan

- Explore with peace of mind. You no longer need to worry about your meal budget during your stay.
- Find a plan to suit you, a choice of Meal Plans for all budgets and palates.
- Add some magic to your stay: some Meal Plans include meals with Disney Characters.
- But don't forget, these plans must be booked before your stay.

How a Meal Plan works?

- Booking: Before you arrive, book the ideal Meal Plan to meet your needs from half board meals to full board meals, from buffets to table service.
- Use: You will receive your meal vouchers upon arrival at the hotel. You will be able to use these vouchers to pay for each meal in the restaurants.

- Restaurants: You will be able to use your vouchers in a selection of more than 20 restaurants, depending on the Meal Plan you've chosen.
- **Please note** that Disneyland Paris Meal Plans are not available for Guests staying at Villages Nature Paris.

- **Smart tip:** Booking your table before you arrive at Disneyland Paris is highly recommended. You can book within the six months before you arrive. Contact the restaurant booking service on **+33 (0)1 60 30 40 50** (international call rates apply). You can also book at the hotel reception.

Our Restaurant Booking Date:

Meal plans

- **Choose your Meal Plan:**

  Breakfast: This includes a delicious breakfast buffet at your hotel (except at Disney's Davy Crockett Ranch where you can collect your breakfast basket from the forest chalet located at the entrance to the bungalow area) per person, for each night of your stay.

  Half board: This includes a breakfast buffet at your hotel & one meal (lunch or dinner) per person, for each night of your stay.

  Full board: This includes a breakfast buffet at your hotel & two meals (lunch and dinner) per person, for each night of your stay.
  Breakfast comprised in special offer with/including free-half-board / full-board dining plans might be served in one of our Disneyland Paris counter service restaurants located In the Disneyland Park or in Walt Disney Studios Park. The name and location of the restaurant will be communicated to you on your arrival.

- **Smart tip:**
- Breakfast is already included in the price of your stay if you book a Suite or a Room at the Castle Club, Empire State Club, Compass Club, Golden Forest Club or at the Algonquin's Explorers Hotel.

- Specific conditions apply to all stays including 24th and 31st December, please contact us or your travel agent.

- **Choose your half-board or full-board plan**

Further information about Disney Meal Plans

- Whatever Meal Plan option you choose, lunch/dinner vouchers are accepted for their monetary value in all restaurants in the Disney Parks and Disney Hotels as well as certain Disney Village restaurants for a meal that includes a starter, main meal and a desert or an all-you-can-eat buffet with a soft drink.
- Breakfast vouchers are also accepted for their monetary value in a selection of restaurants in the Disney Parks and Disney Village, for breakfast only.
- In any case where the total fee exceeds the value of the meal, you will have to pay the difference. No refund will be issued if the total is lower than the value of the meal included in your plan.

Available restaurants	STANDARD	PLUS	PREMIUM
	more than 5	more than 15	more than 20

Breakfast

	STANDARD	PLUS	PREMIUM
🍽 buffet in your hotel	✔	✔	✔
👫 with Disney characters at Plaza Gardens Restaurant	—	—	✔

Lunch / Dinner

	STANDARD	PLUS	PREMIUM
🍽 **Buffet**			
in your hotel²	✔	✔	✔
in the parks and Disney Village	✔	✔	✔
🍴 **Table service**			
with set menu	—	✔	✔
"A la carte"	—	—	✔
👫 **Character Dining**			
Auberge de Cendrillon	—	—	✔
Inventions (except for brunch)	—	—	✔
Café Mickey	—	—	✔
Dinner Show, 2nd seating category "Buffalo Bill's Wild West Show . with Mickey & Friends!"	—	—	✔
🍹 1 soft drink during your meal	✔	✔	✔

Price from

	STANDARD Adult	STANDARD Children (3-11yrs*)	PLUS Adult	PLUS Children (3-11yrs*)	PREMIUM Adult	PREMIUM Children (3-11yrs*)
🛏 **Half Board** Breakfast + 1 meal per person, per night booked	£ 34,31	£ 24,62	£ 48,37	£ 33,42	£ 78,28	£ 54,53
🛏 **Full Board** Breakfast + 2 meals per person, per night booked	£ 51,90	£ 36,94	£ 65,96	£ 45,73	£ 105,54	£ 71,23

Dining Plan example Source correct May 2020
https://www.disneylandparis.com/en-gb/guest-services/meal-plans/

Disneyland Park Dining

Restaurant	Location	Service	Characters	Style
Plaza Gardens	Main Street	Buffet	Breakfast Only	International
Cable Car Bake Shop	Main Street	Quick	no	Snacks
Casey's Corner	Main Street	Quick	no	American
Market House Deli	Main Street	Quick	no	Snacks
Victoria's Home Style	Main Street	Quick	no	Snacks
Walt's American Restaurant	Main Street	Table	no	Fine Dining
Cowboy Cookout BBQ	Frontierland	Hybrid Buffet	no	American
Fuente Del Oro	Frontierland	Quick	no	Tex Mex
Last Chance Cafe	Frontierland	Quick	no	American
Lucky Nugget Saloon	Frontierland	Table	no	Steak & BBQ
Silver Spur Steakhouse	Frontierland	Table	no	Steak & BBQ
Buzz Lightyear's Pizza Planet	Discoveryland	Buffet	no	American
Café Hyperion	Discoveryland	Quick	no	American
Agrabah Cafe	Adventureland	Buffet	no	Mediterranean
Captain Jack's Restaurant des Pirates	Adventureland	Table	no	Seafood
The Coffee Grinder	Main Street	Quick	no	Snacks
Colonel Hathis Pizza Outpost	Adventureland	Quick	no	American
Cookie Kitchen	Main Street	Quick	no	Snacks
Hakuna Matata	Adventureland	Quick	no	African
Au Chalet de la Marionnette	Fantasyland	Quick	no	German

Disneyland Park Dining

Restaurant	Location	Service	Characters	Style
Auberge de Cendrillon	Fantasyland	Table	Yes	Fine Dining
Pizzeria Bella Notte	Fantasyland	Quick	no	Italian
Toad Hall	Fantasyland	Quick	no	British
Ice Cream Company	Main Street	Quick	no	Snacks
Fantasia Gelati	Fantasyland	Quick	no	Ice Cream
Gibson Girl Ice Cream Parlour	Main Street	Quick	no	Ice Cream

Studio Park Dining

Restaurant	Location	Service	Characters	Style
Restaurant En Coulisse	Front Lot	Quick	no	American
Restaurant Des Stars	Courtyard	Buffet	no	International
Blockbuster Cafe	Backlot	Quick	no	American
Café Des Cascadeurs	Backlot	Table	no	American
Bistrot Chez Remy	Place de Remy	Table	no	French Cuisine

Disney Hotel Dining

Restaurant	Location	Service	Characters	Style
Inventions	Disneyland Hotel	Buffet	yes	International
Beaver Creek Tavern	Sequoia Lodge	Table	no	American
California Grill	Disneyland Hotel	Table	no	American
Manhattan	Hotel New York	Table	no	American
Yacht Club	Newport Bay	Table	no	Seafood
Cape Cod	Newport Bay	Buffet	no	Seafood
Chuck wagon cafe	Hotel Cheyenne	Buffet	no	Tex-Mex
Crockett's Tavern	Davy Crockett's Ranch	Buffet	no	International
Hunters Grill	Sequoia Lodge	Buffet	no	International
La Cantina	Santa Fe	Buffet	no	Tex-Mex
Parkside Diner	Hotel New York	Buffet	no	American
Starbucks	Santa Fe & Cheyenne	Quick	no	American

Disney Village Dining

Restaurant	Location	Service	Characters	Style
Annette's Diner	Disney Village	Table	no	American
Café Mickey	Disney Village	Table	yes	International
Buffalo Bills WWS	Disney Village	Table	yes	Tex-Mex
King Ludwigs Castle	Disney Village	Table	no	Bavarian
Planet Hollywood	Disney Village	Table	no	International
Rainforest Cafe	Disney Village	Table	no	International
The Steakhouse	Disney Village	Table	no	American
La Grange at Billy Bobs	Disney Village	Buffet	no	Tex-Mex
Earl of Sandwich	Disney Village	Quick	no	International
McDonalds	Disney Village	Quick	no	American
New York Style Sandwiches	Disney Village	Quick	no	American
Sports Bar	Disney Village	Quick	no	American

Our Table Service Bookings

Restaurant	Date	Time	Location	Meal Plan?

Our Table Service Bookings

Restaurant	Date	Time	Location	Meal Plan?

Our Table Service Bookings

Restaurant	Date	Time	Location	Meal Plan?

Our Table Service Bookings

Restaurant	Date	Time	Location	Meal Plan?

Special Reservations

Example Dessert Parties, Bibbity Bobbity Boutique, Dinner Shows

Date	Event	Location	Pre Paid ?

Quick Service Locations

QS Restaurant	Location	Breakfast / Lunch / Dinner

Quick Service Locations

QS Restaurant	Location	Breakfast / Lunch / Dinner

Quick Service Locations

QS Restaurant	Location	Breakfast / Lunch / Dinner

Quick Service Locations

QS Restaurant	Location	Breakfast / Lunch / Dinner

Snacks We Must Try

Snack Name	Park Location	Sweet / Savoury	Snack Credit ✓

Snacks We Must Try

Snack Name	Park Location	Sweet / Savoury	Snack Credit ✓

Snacks We Must Try

Snack Name	Park Location	Sweet / Savoury	Snack Credit ✓

Snacks We Must Try

Snack Name	Park Location	Sweet / Savoury	Snack Credit ✓

Characters We Want to Meet

Character	Park / Resort Location	Fast Pass ✓	Photographer Present ✓

Characters We Want to Meet

Character	Park / Resort Location	Fast Pass ✓	Photographer Present ✓

Notes

_____

_____

_____

_____

_____

_____

_____

_____

_____

_____

_____

_____

_____

_____

_____

_____

_____

_____

_____

_____

Notes

_____
_____
_____
_____
_____
_____
_____
_____
_____
_____
_____
_____
_____
_____
_____
_____
_____
_____
_____
_____

Ride Fastpass Options

At Disneyland Paris you can make free Fastpass reservations using one of the Fastpass ticket machines usually beside the Fastpassable ride. The ticket will give you a return time slot of when you can queue in the Fastpass entrance.

Information from https://www.disneylandparis.com/en-gb/guest-services/fast-pass/

Correct as of May 2020

You Can Use Disneyland Paris FASTPASS on the Following Attractions:

DISNEYLAND PARK

   Indiana Jones and the Temple of Peril, Adventureland

   Star Wars: Hyperspace Mountain, Discoveryland

   Buzz Lightyear Laser Blast*, Discoveryland

   Big Thunder Mountain, Frontierland

   Peter Pan's Flight, Fantasyland

   Star Tours, Discoveryland

WALT DISNEY STUDIOS PARK

    The Twilight Zone Tower of Terror**, Production Courtyard

       Ratatouille: The Adventure, Toon Studio

Smart Tip

You can only have one FASTPASS ticket at a time per person. Another ticket can only be obtained once the previous one has been used or 2 hours after the previous one. The FASTPASS ticket is only used with a Disney Park admission ticket valid for the same day. The distribution of FASTPASS tickets is subject to the availability of the service and tickets.

Super & Ultimate Fastpass Options

Fastpass ticket options can be purchased for an additional daily price to beat the queues, these may be a good option if you are visiting in the busy season.

	SUPER FASTPASS		ULTIMATE FASTPASS	
	FAMILY ATTRACTIONS	BIG THRILL ATTRACTIONS	ALL FASTPASS ATTRACTIONS	ALL FASTPASS ATTRACTIONS
	ONE TIME SPEEDY ACCESS	ONE TIME SPEEDY ACCESS	ONE TIME SPEEDY ACCESS	UNLIMITED SPEEDY ACCESS
Ratatouille: The Adventure	✓		✓	✓
Peter Pan's Flight	✓		✓	✓
Buzz Lightyear Laser Blast	✓		✓	✓
Star Wars Hyperspace Mountain		✓	✓	✓
Phantom Manor		✓	✓	✓
The Twilight Zone Tower of Terror		✓	✓	✓
Big Thunder Mountain			✓	✓
Star Tours: The Adventures Continue			✓	✓
Indiana Jones and the Temple of Peril			✓	✓
Low/High season Prices per person, per day	£26,39 / £39,58	£26,39 / £39,58	£52,77 / £79,16	£105,54 / £131,93

FASTPASS ATTRACTIONS

Rides we want to ride

Date and Park	Ride	Location	FP?

Rides we want to ride

Date and Park	Ride	Location	FP?

Rides we want to ride

Date and Park	Ride	Location	FP?

Rides we want to ride

Date and Park	Ride	Location	FP?

Rides we want to ride

Date and Park	Ride	Location	FP?

Rides we want to ride

Date and Park	Ride	Location	FP?

Rides we want to ride

Date and Park	Ride	Location	FP?

Rides we want to ride

Date and Park	Ride	Location	FP?

Notes

_____

_____

_____

_____

_____

_____

_____

_____

_____

_____

_____

_____

_____

_____

_____

_____

_____

_____

_____

_____

Shows and Parades

Park	Show Name	Time

Photopass 'Magic' Character Locations

Park	Location	Photo Type

Things left to do

✓ ☐

1. _____ ☐
2. _____ ☐
3. _____ ☐
4. _____ ☐
5. _____ ☐
6. _____ ☐
7. _____ ☐
8. _____ ☐
9. _____ ☐
10. _____ ☐
11. _____ ☐
12. _____ ☐

Things left to do

✓ ☐

1. _____ ☐
2. _____ ☐
3. _____ ☐
4. _____ ☐
5. _____ ☐
6. _____ ☐
7. _____ ☐
8. _____ ☐
9. _____ ☐
10. _____ ☐
11. _____ ☐
12. _____ ☐

Packing List

✓ ☐

1. _____ ☐
2. _____ ☐
3. _____ ☐
4. _____ ☐
5. _____ ☐
6. _____ ☐
7. _____ ☐
8. _____ ☐
9. _____ ☐
10. _____ ☐
11. _____ ☐
12. _____ ☐

Packing List

✓ ☐

1. _____ ☐
2. _____ ☐
3. _____ ☐
4. _____ ☐
5. _____ ☐
6. _____ ☐
7. _____ ☐
8. _____ ☐
9. _____ ☐
10. _____ ☐
11. _____ ☐
12. _____ ☐

Notes

_____

_____

_____

_____

_____

_____

_____

_____

_____

_____

_____

_____

_____

_____

_____

_____

_____

_____

_____

Daily Trip Planner

Daily Planner

Date & Day: _____	Park or Activities	Food Plans
AM		
PM		

Things to Pack:

_____

_____

Daily Planner

Date & Day: _____	Park or Activities	Food Plans
AM		
PM		

Things to Pack:

_____

_____

Daily Planner

Date & Day: _____	Park or Activities	Food Plans
AM		
PM		

Things to Pack:

_____

_____

Daily Planner

Date & Day: _____	Park or Activities	Food Plans
AM		
PM		

Things to Pack:

_____

_____

Daily Planner

Date & Day: _____	Park or Activities	Food Plans
AM		
PM		

Things to Pack:

_____

_____

Daily Planner

Date & Day: _____	Park or Activities	Food Plans
AM		
PM		

Things to Pack:

_____

_____

Daily Planner

Date & Day: _____	Park or Activities	Food Plans
AM		
PM		

Things to Pack:

_____

_____

Daily Planner

Date & Day: _____	Park or Activities	Food Plans
AM		
PM		

Things to Pack:

_____

_____

Daily Planner

Date & Day: _____	Park or Activities	Food Plans
AM		
PM		

Things to Pack:

_____

_____

Daily Planner

Date & Day: _____	Park or Activities	Food Plans
AM		
PM		

Things to Pack:

_____

_____

Daily Planner

Date & Day: _____	Park or Activities	Food Plans
AM		
PM		

Things to Pack:

_____

_____

Daily Planner

Date & Day: -----------------	Park or Activities	Food Plans
AM		
PM		

Things to Pack:

_____

_____

Daily Planner

Date & Day: _____	Park or Activities	Food Plans
AM		
PM		

Things to Pack:

_____

_____

Daily Planner

Date & Day: _____	Park or Activities	Food Plans
AM		
PM		

Things to Pack:

_____

_____

Daily Planner

Date & Day: ----------------	Park or Activities	Food Plans
AM		
PM		

Things to Pack:

_____

_____

Daily Trip Journal

Day 1: Date

_____

_____

_____

_____

_____

_____

_____

_____

_____

_____

_____

Favourite part of the day:

_____

Favourite meal or snack:

_____

Day 2: Date

_____

_____

_____

_____

_____

_____

_____

_____

_____

_____

_____

_____

_____

Favourite part of the day:

_____

Favourite meal or snack:

_____

Day 3: Date

_____

_____

_____

_____

_____

_____

_____

_____

_____

_____

_____

_____

_____

Favourite part of the day:

_____

Favourite meal or snack:

_____

Day 4: Date

_____

_____

_____

_____

_____

_____

_____

_____

_____

_____

_____

_____

Favourite part of the day:

_____

Favourite meal or snack:

_____

Day 5: Date

_____
_____
_____
_____
_____
_____
_____
_____
_____
_____
_____

Favourite part of the day:

_____

Favourite meal or snack:

_____

Day 6: Date

_____

_____

_____

_____

_____

_____

_____

_____

_____

_____

_____

_____

_____

Favourite part of the day:

_____

Favourite meal or snack:

_____

Day 7: Date

_____
_____
_____
_____
_____
_____
_____
_____
_____
_____
_____
_____

Favourite part of the day:

_____

Favourite meal or snack:

_____

Day 8: Date

_____

_____

_____

_____

_____

_____

_____

_____

_____

_____

_____

_____

_____

Favourite part of the day:

_____

Favourite meal or snack:

_____

Day 9: Date

_____

_____

_____

_____

_____

_____

_____

_____

_____

_____

_____

_____

Favourite part of the day:

_____

Favourite meal or snack:

_____

Day 10: Date

_____
_____
_____
_____
_____
_____
_____
_____
_____
_____
_____
_____
_____

Favourite part of the day:

_____

Favourite meal or snack:

_____

Day 11: Date

_____

_____

_____

_____

_____

_____

_____

_____

_____

_____

_____

Favourite part of the day:

_____

Favourite meal or snack:

_____

Day 12: Date

_____

_____

_____

_____

_____

_____

_____

_____

_____

_____

_____

_____

Favourite part of the day:

_____

Favourite meal or snack:

_____

Day 13: Date

_____

_____

_____

_____

_____

_____

_____

_____

_____

_____

_____

_____

Favourite part of the day:

_____

Favourite meal or snack:

_____

Day 14: Date

_____
_____
_____
_____
_____
_____
_____
_____
_____
_____
_____
_____
_____

Favourite part of the day:

_____

Favourite meal or snack:

_____

Day 15: Date

_____
_____
_____
_____
_____
_____
_____
_____
_____
_____
_____
_____

Favourite part of the day:

_____

Favourite meal or snack:

_____

Notes

_____
_____
_____
_____
_____
_____
_____
_____
_____
_____
_____
_____
_____
_____
_____
_____
_____
_____

Notes

_____
_____
_____
_____
_____
_____
_____
_____
_____
_____
_____
_____
_____
_____
_____
_____
_____
_____
_____